NO LONGER PROPERTY OF
SEATTLE PUBLIC LIBRARY

Received

OCT

D0554890

NATIVE NATIONS OF THE
GREAT BASIN
AND PLATEAU

BY BARBARA KRASNER

The Child's World

Published by The Child's World®
1980 Lookout Drive • Mankato, MN 56003-1705
800-599-READ • www.childsworld.com

Acknowledgments
The Child's World®: Mary Berendes, Publishing Director
Red Line Editorial: Editorial direction and production
The Design Lab: Design
Content Consultant: Caskey Russell, Director, American Indian
Studies, University of Wyoming

Photographs ©: Elaine Thompson/AP Images, cover, 2; Brooklyn
Museum/Corbis, 1, 32; Kris Holland/Yakima Herald-Republic/
AP Images, 3 (top), 14; HES Photography/Shutterstock Images,
3 (middle top), 20; Taylor Goforth/U.S. Fish and Wildlife Service
Pacific Region, 3 (middle bottom), 15, 16; Patrick McCully CC
2.0, 3 (bottom), 36; John A. Anderson/Shutterstock Images, 5;
Public Domain, 6, 21; Marilyn Angel Wynn/Nativestock Pictures/
Corbis, 7, 10, 22, 25; Smithsonian Institution/U.S. National
Archives and Records Administration, 8; Mason Trinca/Yakima
Herald-Republic/AP Images, 9; Everett Historical/Shutterstock
Images, 11, 13; Troy Maben/AP Images, 12; Charles Rex Arbogast/
AP Images, 18; Gary Potts/Shutterstock Images, 23; John Miller/
AP Images, 26; U.S. Department of Agriculture, 27; Allyson
Mathis/U.S. National Park Service, 29; Shutterstock Images, 30,
39; Library of Congress, 31; Allen Cole/U.S. Fish and Wildlife
Service Pacific Region, 33; U.S. Fish and Wildlife Service, 34

Copyright © 2016 by The Child's World®
All rights reserved. No part of this book may be
reproduced or utilized in any form or by any means
without written permission from the publisher.
ISBN: 9781634070317
LCCN: 2014959802
Printed in the United States of America
Mankato, MN
July, 2015
PA02269

ABOUT THE AUTHOR

Freelance author Barbara Krasner writes nonfiction, fiction, and poetry for children and adults. She holds an MFA in Writing for Children & Young Adults from the Vermont College of Fine Arts and teaches children's literature and creative writing at William Paterson University in New Jersey, where she is currently pursuing a master's in public history.

A rider participates in a ceremony remembering the 1877–1878 imprisonment of a peaceful Nez Percé band.

TABLE OF CONTENTS

ARCTIC
OCEAN

GREENLAND

Gulf of
Alaska

CANADA

Hudson
Bay

PACIFIC

OCEAN

ATLANTIC

OCEAN

UNITED STATES

MEXICO

Gulf of
Mexico

KEY

GREAT BASIN AND PLATEAU
NATIVE NATIONS

N
W   E
S

4

CHAPTER ONE

GREAT BASIN AND PLATEAU NATIVE NATIONS

The Great Basin and plateau region stretches across ten states. Its borders in the west lie in Washington, Oregon, and California. Its borders in the east are in Wyoming and Colorado. At the northern end is Montana. At the southern tip are

The Great Basin and plateau region has tall mountains and dramatic canyons.

Nevada and Arizona. In between are Idaho and Utah. The region also includes the plateau near the mighty Columbia and Colorado rivers. The region has the Cascade, Rocky, and Uinta mountain ranges. In the area's deserts, summer temperatures soar and winter temperatures drop.

Many Native Nations call this geographic area home. They include the Nez Percé, Yakama, Shoshone-Bannock, Ute, Paiute, Washoe, and Klamath. Native Peoples have lived in the Great Basin and plateau region for thousands of years. Groups moved with the seasons to hunt and gather certain foods. When the weather turned cold, they settled into winter villages where they had previously stored food. These villages were near water and wood. They were close to the mouths of canyons or along streams filled with fish.

Ute doll, ca. 1905

Many groups hunted and ate **pronghorn**, deer, jackrabbits, and wild sheep. They caught and ate salmon. Some groups grew crops year-round.

Most of the nations of the Great Basin share similar languages. The languages belong to a language family called Numic. The Comanche of the southern plains, whose home was once the Great Basin, speak a similar language. One nation, the Washoe, speaks a different language type, Hokan.

In the nineteenth century, the Native Nations of the Great Basin and plateau were forced to sign treaties with the U.S. government. In these contracts, the U.S. government promised Native Nations protection from attacks. The agreements promised hunting and fishing rights for generations to come. The U.S.

A Nez Percé woman attends a powwow.

A Shoshone group visited Washington, D.C., in the late nineteenth century, likely to discuss treaty rights.

government recognized the nations' right to govern themselves. This right is known as **sovereignty**. Most nations gained federal recognition. This means the U.S. government formed a relationship with the nations' governments. Through the treaties, the U.S. government gained land previously belonging to the Native Nations. However,

The region's Native Peoples hold ceremonies to bless their traditional food sources as the seasons change. The Yakama and Warm Springs (formerly known as Walla Walla) groups hold a Salmon Feast in the spring and a Huckleberry Feast in summer. **Oral histories** say the salmon and the huckleberry offered themselves to the Creator to become food for people.

A Yakama biologist teaches students about raising salmon. The nation works to conserve the salmon population.

many nations, even more than 100 years later, struggle with the terms and unbroken promises of these treaties.

During the nineteenth and twentieth centuries, the U.S. government made it illegal for Native Peoples to practice aspects of their religion and culture, including dancing. Activists throughout the country fought the laws. In 1978, President Jimmy Carter signed the American Indian Religious Freedom Act. This allowed Native Peoples to practice their traditional religions once more.

Many nations of the Great Basin and plateau govern themselves through councils. The nations run businesses to earn money. They grow crops, raise cattle, run **casinos**, and craft artwork such as baskets. Programs encourage nation members to practice their traditional cultures. These include language instruction, museums, and festivals.

CHAPTER TWO

NEZ PERCÉ

The Nez Percé once lived in northeastern Oregon. French settlers gave them the name Nez Percé. The name means "pierced nose." They call themselves *Nimi'ipuu*, which means "the people."

Riders travel the Nez Percé Trail to commemorate a battle of the Nez Percé War in the 1870s.

Nez Percé family, ca. 1909

The Nez Percé signed a treaty with the U.S. government in the 1850s. In the 1870s, the government forced them to move onto **reservations**. Before that, they lived in **bands** near rivers and streams. They once lived in longhouses and then **tepees**. Now they live in modern housing but still use the tepee for camping.

Nez Percé leader Anthony Johnson speaks about a water-use agreement designed to protect salmon in the Snake River Basin.

In 2011, approximately 3,500 Nez Percé lived on the Nez Percé Indian Reservation in Idaho. They run a program along the Columbia, Snake, Clearwater, and other rivers to protect the fish. They manage and protect their forests and sell wood and forest products. They also run the Clearwater River Casino & Lodge.

Salmon have always been important to the Nez Percé. Salmon shape Nez Percé culture and religion. For nearly 100 years, dams have threatened the rivers where salmon come to lay their eggs. With fewer salmon available, the Nez Percé also lose an important part of their diet. In 1986, scientists realized the coho type of salmon no longer existed in

One of the most famous Nez Percé leaders is Chief Joseph. He led a group of Nez Percé during the 1870s. During this time, some groups moved to the reservation in Idaho while others tried to stay in their homes. His group began traveling to the reservation, but some young men fought with white settlers. The U.S. Army chased his group for 1,400 miles (2,250 km). They fought several battles despite being outnumbered. But ultimately Chief Joseph's group surrendered in 1877.

Chief Joseph

Idaho rivers. The Nez Percé took action. Nez Percé biologists took special care to hatch eggs found in a section of the Columbia River and made sure the young salmon could survive. Their strategies combine ancient knowledge with cutting-edge science.

Many Nez Percé live on the Colville Reservation in Washington, too. They share the land with 11 other tribes. These peoples were all living in the same area when Fort Colville was built in the early nineteenth century. They are now known as Confederated Tribes of the Colville Reservation. Their population is approximately 9,000. They run more than a dozen businesses, including **gaming**, tourism, and forest products. These businesses are important to the region's economy.

CHAPTER THREE

YAKAMA

*Children of the Yakama Nation perform a dance at an event celebrating
the release of salmon into Lake Cle Elum in Washington.*

The Yakama Nation settled along the Columbia River in central Washington's plateau region below the Cascade Mountains. Today more than 10,000 members live on the Yakama Indian Reservation in Washington.

A Yakama Nation member uses a dip net to fish for salmon in the Klickitat River.

The Yakama Nation has 14 separate bands. The Yakama council includes representatives from each of these bands. The council helps make sure Yakama rights are protected.

It oversees the finances and well-being of the Yakama, as well as education and housing. The Yakama council was created in 1944 and is a unique form of government. A general

Yakama Nation members celebrate the removal of a dam in 2011.

council includes all nation members aged 18 and older. They elect council representatives. Twenty years ago, the nation changed its name from Yakima to Yakama to come closer to its actual pronunciation. The council voted on this decision and made it a reality.

The Yakama speak a dialect of the Sahaptin language. Several Native Nations of the plateau speak this language, including the Nez Percé. The Yakama Nation offers a language program so young people can learn its dialect.

Yakama businesses include the Legends Casino and gaming, a resort, and natural resources such as land, wildlife, and energy. Nation members sell fruit and vegetables. A cultural center has a museum and a theater. It hosts several special events every year, including a day in August when Yakama youth volunteer in their community.

The nation has been active in preserving First Foods. First Foods are traditional foods in the Yakama diet, such as deer, salmon, roots, berries, and water. The Yakama use these foods for weddings, funerals, and other religious and cultural reasons. But dams in the area threaten food production. Similar to the Nez Percé, the Yakama are taking special actions to restore salmon to the rivers. They hatch salmon eggs and then place young salmon into the water every spring.

Each year the Yakama celebrate the signing of the Treaty of 1855. The treaty guarantees their rights to hunt, fish, and gather. They hold a **powwow** and a parade. The celebration includes a rodeo, golf tournament, softball tournament, and salmon bake. There is also a dance exhibition. The powwow lasts several days. People sell arts and crafts such as jewelry and beadwork. They also sell traditional foods such as frybread and Indian tacos. Frybread is made from flour, baking powder, salt, milk, and water. The dough is mixed and fried to a golden brown. It is often then topped with honey, cinnamon, or sugar. It is also used for Indian tacos, which have ground beef, lettuce, tomatoes, and other ingredients as the filling.

SAY IT		
sun	áan	(on)
moon	álxayx	(al-khaykh)
water	chúush	(chush)

CHAPTER FOUR

SHOSHONE-BANNOCK

Sacagawea statue, Idaho. In the background, people watch a history reenactment at the Sacagawea Center during Sacagawea Heritage Days.

The Shoshone-Bannock are two different peoples. They speak different languages. Yet they share similar cultures. Sacagawea, the woman who helped guide Meriwether Lewis and William Clark in their northwestern expedition in the early 1800s, was a member of the Shoshone Nation.

Sacagawea was kidnapped and taken away from her family by the Hidatsa tribe. She was approximately ten years old. Later a French Canadian fur trapper, Toussaint Charbonneau, bought her to be his wife. Meriwether Lewis and William Clark hired Charbonneau to be an interpreter for them as they headed west to the Pacific Ocean. Sacagawea was important to the expedition. Having a Native woman with the group showed the people they met that they were peaceful. Sacagawea's son, called Pomp, was born on the journey. When the group reached Shoshone lands, Sacagawea was reunited with her brother. He sold them horses to help them on their journey. Sacagawea returned to the Hidatsa village with Charbonneau and her son at the end of the expedition. History does not know exactly what happened to her next or when she died.

The Shoshone and Bannock signed a treaty with the United States in 1868 to make peace with the U.S. government. The treaty protected Shoshone and Bannock rights to hunt and fish. But in exchange, the groups had to give up much of their traditional land. The treaty created the Fort Hall Reservation in southeastern Idaho. Groups that did not want to move were forced to anyway. Today, approximately 4,000 members live there.

The Shoshone-Bannock are known for the Shoshone-Bannock Festival held each year in August. Tribal members hold a powwow, rodeo, softball game, and arts and crafts show. The sport of Indian relay horse racing began on the Fort Hall Reservation more than 100 years ago. Relay racers ride bareback. Each team has three horses and four team members. Only one member actually rides the horses. The rider must complete one lap with each horse. Other team members hold the horses. The event

Relay race at Fort Hall Reservation

has become a tradition, with multiple generations of families racing.

Beading is a tradition in the Shoshone-Bannock Nation. It has been passed down from generation to generation for centuries. Beadwork is intended to tell a story. Beadwork can include symbols and figures that have particular meaning to the tribe's origins, beliefs, and oral histories. Some of it is worn as jewelry. Much of Shoshone-Bannock beadwork features flower designs. A rose typically stands for the Shoshone-Bannock. Artists sell their beadwork through reservation shops and on the Internet.

Shoshone-Bannock members run a number of businesses, including three casinos, a gift shop, a hotel and event center, tribal farms, an online news service, and

Shoshone moccasins with beadwork, ca. 1900

natural gas drilling. For more than 40 years, the tribe ran a mining business. Now gaming helps bring money back into the tribe.

CHAPTER FIVE

UTE

The Ute Fish and Wildlife Department watches over natural resources in the Uintah and Ouray Reservation in Utah.

Seven Ute bands live on three reservations in Utah, Colorado, and New Mexico. The Ute were not a unified people historically. The Northern Ute live on the Uintah and Ouray Reservation in Utah. It is the second-largest reservation in the United

States. It has more than 4.5 million acres (1.8 million ha). Approximately one-half of their membership of 3,000 live there. The Northern Utes run several businesses including gas stations, a bowling alley, and a supermarket. Much of the nation's earnings come from raising cattle, agriculture, and oil drilling. Natural gas production is also big business. The Southern Ute live in Colorado and have approximately 1,400 **enrolled** members. This group produces oil and gas and runs the Sky Ute Casino.

The third reservation, Ute Mountain Reservation, is located at the point where Colorado, Utah, and New Mexico meet. Approximately 2,000 members live there. They make their living through farming, ranching, tourism, gaming, and pottery. Since 1973, the Ute have been encouraging their

A dancer performs at Ute Mountain Reservation.

artists to create their traditional, unique, hand-painted pottery. Many pots have geometric black and white designs. Pottery has been part of Ute culture since the times of their ancient ancestors. Pieces of finely decorated handicrafts have been discovered in the ruins of ancient buildings and villages. Today, Ute Mountain Indian Pottery sells its products to the public.

Each spring, the Ute hold the Bear Dance ceremony. According to oral tradition, two brothers went out to hunt. They stopped to rest. One saw an upright bear dancing and singing around a tree. While one brother continued to hunt, the other watched the bear. The bear taught him the dance and a song to go with it. The bear told the man to go back to his people and teach them. Today, the bear dance reminds the Ute of the bear's spirit and strength. For the dance, women wear shawls and wave the fringes at the men, inviting them to dance. All the men are on one side and the women are on the other. The women move first and then they step back and forth. Later in the dance, the men and women break the lines and form couples. Instead of drums, musicians play rasps, which produce a grating sound, much like a bear clawing and growling.

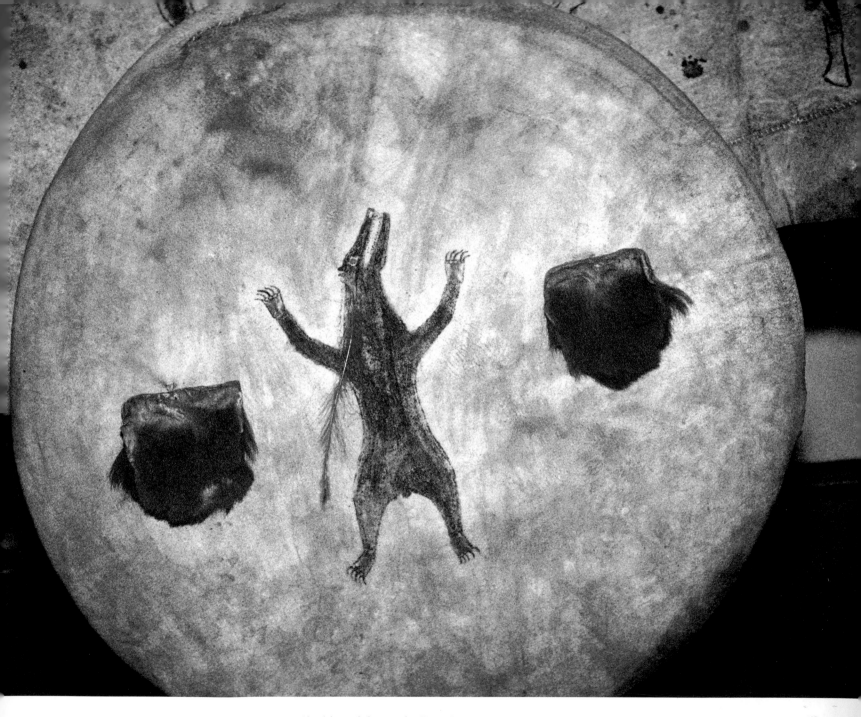

Shield used during the Bear Dance ceremony

CHAPTER SIX

PAIUTE

The Paiute include the Northern Paiute, Owens Valley Paiute, and Southern Paiute. The Northern Paiute live in the Great Basin region in California, Nevada, Idaho, and Oregon. They are related to the Shoshone and speak a different language than the Southern Paiute.

Northern Paiute and Shoshone residents of the Duck Valley Reservation allow visitors to pay to fish in their waterways.

The Paiute members of Pyramid Lake Reservation work with the U.S. Department of Agriculture to improve harvests.

The Owens Valley Paiute once lived near Owens River on the south side of the Sierra Nevada mountain range. They also speak the Shoshone language. Today they live on several reservations in California and Nevada.

Fifteen bands of the Southern Paiute live in Nevada, Utah, and Arizona. They number approximately 14,000 people. They have a shared background with the Ute. The Southern Paiute are well known for basket weaving. Their tightly stitched baskets are made from willow reeds. The baskets are often covered with colorful glass beads.

The Southern Paiute experienced an event during the mid-twentieth century that was common for many nations. At that time, the U.S. government declared that certain Native Nations and bands no longer officially existed. The government insisted these peoples had fully **assimilated** into

U.S. culture and no longer needed to be separately recognized. This was a trend called **termination**. Four Southern Paiute bands were officially ended by the U.S. government in 1954. This left them with no health care, land, or government funding. They fell into poverty and despair. In the 1950s and 1960s, they fought for land in the courts, and they won some cases. They regained federal recognition in 1980. They also received U.S. funding to bring services and businesses to the bands. Four years later, their land was restored.

The Cedar Breaks National Monument, part of the National Park Service, honors and protects Southern Paiute history. It includes the Markagunt Plateau, where Southern Paiute gathered berries and plants and hunted deer and elk. In this area, archaeologists also discovered Southern Paiute stone tools and pieces of pottery. According to Southern Paiute oral history, the odd-shaped rock monuments, called hoodoos, contain frozen people.

The language of the Southern Paiute has not been written down. Few members speak it fully. There are efforts to try to revive it. This is a situation common to many Native Nations. The Paiute Indian Tribe of Utah has a "Seven Generations Goal." It wants to preserve the nation's culture and traditions in a museum and cultural center, thinking seven generations, or nearly 200 years, into the future.

			SAY IT
one	sumu'yoo	(seem-e-yoo)	
two	waha'yoo	(was-ha-yoo)	
three	pahe'yoo	(pah-ee-yoo)	

*Southern Paiute and other Native Nations representatives meet with archaeologists
at the Grand Canyon to discuss findings from an excavation.*

CHAPTER SEVEN

WASHOE

Lake Tahoe serves as the cultural and spiritual center for the Washoe Nation of Nevada and California. In the mid-nineteenth century, the California Gold Rush and then a silver rush in Nevada disrupted the Washoe way of life. Because of miners, immigrants, and the new logging industry, the Washoe lost much of their forests,

The Washoe Nation has lived near Lake Tahoe for untold generations.

Washoe member Dat So La Lee (ca. 1835–1925) was a famous basket maker. Museums in Nevada and the Smithsonian Institution in Washington, D.C., show samples of her work. She made approximately 300 baskets. Today one of her baskets can sell for $1,000,000. Baskets such as hers, with flat bases and small openings, were used to hold soups, drinks, and foods. They were also used in ceremonies and dances.

Basket maker Dat So La Lee

fishing, and hunting. They suffered from starvation. Through this new contact with nonnatives, they suffered from disease. They were pushed out of their lands.

By 1880, Washoe leaders began to petition the government for land. They finally won back some land in 1917. But the Washoe continued to fight for land until the 1970s when their claim was settled.

Today, approximately 1,500 members are enrolled. A council on the reservation at Lake Tahoe manages the group's affairs. The council includes representatives from four Washoe communities located outside Lake Tahoe.

Basket by Dat So La Lee, early twentieth century

The nation runs the Meeks Bay Resort and Marina on the shores of Lake Tahoe. The Washoe celebrate an annual Pine Nut Festival, which honors the traditional fall pine nut harvest. The ceremony dates back at least 100 years. Pine nuts were an important source of food during the long winter months. The Washoe also hold an annual Wa-She-Shu-It-Deh ("The People from Here") arts and crafts festival. The festival has competitions for arts and crafts such as basket weaving. People come to drum and dance and eat Native foods, too.

CHAPTER EIGHT

KLAMATH

A 2003 Klamath research project studied the mule deer population in south-central Oregon using tracking collars.

An 1864 treaty with the U.S. government created the Klamath Reservation in Oregon. The Klamath have three bands: Klamath, Modoc, and Yahooskin. Through the treaty, the Klamath were able to keep their forests, which are important to their

Klamath Nation children learn to combine cultural knowledge about the local environment with high-tech tools and scientific methods.

economy. The Klamath became the second-wealthiest Native Nation in the United States by the middle of the twentieth century. Many nations, but not the Klamath, were living in poverty. The U.S. government then sought to do away with nations and reservations altogether. The Klamath Nation was officially terminated in 1954. The federal government took back the land. The nation was restored in 1986, and today it has a 566-acre (230 ha) reservation.

Until the middle of the twentieth century, many Native children, including the Klamath, received their education at boarding schools or mission schools. The U.S. and Canadian governments set up these schools beginning in the 1880s. Many children were forced to attend. There they had to give up their traditional culture and language. It was a painful time for many. Traditions were lost, and children grew up without speaking their language. Some of these schools continue, but today they teach students to honor their culture.

The Klamath have approximately 3,500 enrolled members. To help keep their traditions alive, they run a culture camp for the young and teach the Klamath language. They are building a museum and cultural center.

SAY IT		
father	ptisap	(pee-sa)
fire	loloqs	(loh-lohks)
beaver	pom	(pohm)
ice	wes	(wehs)
dried fish	qamals	(kahm-ahls)

Klamath protesters call for removing the Klamath River dam.

For three days each summer, the Klamath celebrate their official restoration. Activities include a run/walk, powwow, parade, youth rodeo, and barbeque. The Klamath view it as a way for children, parents, and grandparents to learn and honor history and tradition together. They welcome outside visitors to share these traditions.

The 1997 construction of a casino was the first Klamath enterprise since termination and restoration. The casino attracts 300,000 visitors a year. The Klamath also run a travel center and store.

Similar to the Nez Percé and Yakama, the Klamath rely on salmon for their diet. But dams across rivers block the fish from returning home to **spawn**. The Klamath are working to get the government to un-dam the Klamath River.

Natural resources are important to the Klamath. Their economy has been based on timber and agriculture. Termination, however, made it difficult for them to earn a living. The nation's restoration enabled the Klamath to start a gaming business.

assimilated (uh-SIM-uh-late-id) People who have assimilated have become part of a different culture than their own. The U.S. government encouraged Native Peoples to give up their culture and become assimilated into white culture.

bands (BANDZ) Bands are small groups of members of a Native Nation. Native Peoples of the Great Basin and Plateau often lived as smaller bands.

casinos (cah-SEEN-ohs) Casinos are businesses where visitors go to play games of chance for money. Many Native Nations run casinos to make money and provide jobs for their members.

enrolled (en-ROHLD) To be enrolled in a Native Nation means to apply for membership and be accepted. Some enrolled members live on reservations but some do not.

gaming (GEY-ming) Gaming is another word for gambling. Many Native Nations support their local economies through gaming businesses.

oral histories (AWR-uhl HIS-tuh-rees) Oral histories are the history and memories of a people told out loud. Oral histories might tell how Native Peoples came to live on their lands.

powwow (POU-wouw) A powwow is a social gathering of Native Americans that usually includes dancing. Many Native Nations have powwows to celebrate their culture and traditions.

pronghorn (PRAWNG-hawrn) A pronghorn is an animal that resembles an antelope. Native Peoples have long hunted pronghorn for food.

reservations (rez-er-VAY-shuhns) Reservations are areas of land set aside for Native American use. Reservations are run by their own governments and provide services to their residents.

sovereignty (SOV-rin-tee) Sovereignty is the independent power to govern. Tribal sovereignty grants Native Nations the right to govern themselves.

spawn (SPAWN) To spawn is to produce. Salmon and other fish swim upstream to spawn, unless a dam prevents them.

tepees (TEE-pees) Tepees are cone-shaped tents made of animal skins. Some Great Basin and Plateau Nation members lived in tepees.

termination (TUR-muh-ney-shun) Loss of official recognition of a tribe as the result of U.S. government policy was called termination. The Klamath tribe lost rights and privileges as a result of its termination.

BOOKS

Doherty, Craig A. and Katherine M. Doherty. *Plateau Indians.* New York: Chelsea House/ Infobase Publishing, 2008.

Johnson, Michael and Duncan Clarke. *Native Tribes of the Great Basin and Plateau.* Milwaukee, WI: World Almanac Library, 2004.

WEB SITES

Visit our Web site for links about Native Nations of the Great Basin and Plateau:
childsworld.com/links

Note to Parents, Teachers, and Librarians: We routinely verify our Web links to make sure they are safe and active sites. So encourage your readers to check them out!